FAIRACRES PUBLICATIONS 226

SIGNS OF THE TIMES

A Brief Survey of the Bible's Apocalpytic Writings

Tony Dickinson

SLG Press

© 2025 SLG Press
First edition 2025

FAIRACRES PUBLICATIONS 226

ISBN 978-0-7283-0418-5
Fairacres Publications Series ISSN 0307-1405

SLG Press asserts the right of Tony Dickinson to be identified as the author of this work, in accordance with the Copyright Designs and Patents act, 1988.

All rights reserved. No part of this publication may be reproduced, stored in a retrieval system, or transmitted, in any form or by any means, electronic, mechanical, photocopying, recording or otherwise, without the prior permission of the copyright owner.

The publishers have no control over, or responsibility for, any third-party website referred to in this book. All internet addresses given in this book were correct at the time of going to press. The authors and publisher regret any inconvenience caused if addresses have changed or sites have ceased to exist, but can accept no responsibility for any such changes.

Edited and typeset in Palatino Linotype by Julia Craig-McFeely

Biblical quotations are taken from the New Revised Standard Version of the Bible unless otherwise noted.

Cover image: detail from a photograph 2014 by Dennis G. Jarvis of part of the Angers Apocalypse, reproduced under the Creative Commons Attribution-Share Alike 2.0 Generic license

SLG Press
Convent of the Incarnation
Fairacres • Oxford
www.slgpress.co.uk

Printed by
Grosvenor Group Ltd, Loughton, Essex

CONTENTS

Foreword	iii
Introduction	1
Deciphering Daniel	3
Grappling with the Gospels	10
A Reading of Revelation	17
Postscript	29
Suggested Further Reading	32

Foreword

The original version of these reflections on the books of the Bible which are usually lumped together under the heading of 'Apocalyptic', was written as a guide for people in search of some sort of direction during the weeks leading up to Advent 1999, as the second Christian millennium drew to its close. Then, as now, there was a sense that things could not go on as they had been and some of the manifestations of that unease are comparable. There were widespread demonstrations—but against capitalist excess, in those days, rather than governmental indifference to a cost-of-living crisis and climate catastrophe. There was conflict in the Balkans and in Chechnya. There were earthquakes and high-profile killings.

Many other things were different a quarter of a century ago. It was before '9/11' and the wars in Iraq and Afghanistan, before the attempt by 'Islamic State'[1] to bring a Salafist Caliphate into being on the back of the Syrian civil war.[2] It was long before politics across much of Europe, not to mention the USA, had curdled into xenophobia and culture wars. Although the armed conflict within and between the successor states of the former Yugoslavia had only recently ended, there was no thought that a major European war such as the one which has been unfolding in Ukraine since February 2022 was remotely likely, and it was long before anyone other than the seriously 'green', and the committed followers of the way of St Francis of Assisi, were more than slightly concerned about environmental degradation and climate change.

The main 'signs of the times' *then* were the sort of generalized millennial angst which first prompted my ponderings, and trouble

---

[1] Otherwise known as Da'esh.
[2] An ultra-conservative fundamentalist movement within Sunni Islam.

once again in the Middle East. On the other hand, a group of Charismatic Catholic musicians and speakers in the town where I ministered in those days was turning down engagements in 2000 and beyond because their leader expected the Lord's imminent return. Large numbers of people were convinced anything controlled by a computer would explode and, as might have been expected, Jehovah's Witnesses were busily attempting to share with anyone who would listen those passages from the Bible which, according to their worldview, are telling those who sign up to it exactly what God is planning to do about the apparently hopeless mess that constitutes the world in which we live.

It is a reasonable assumption that 'those passages from the Bible' will come from one of three areas:

- the later writings included in the Hebrew Scriptures—and most likely from the book attributed to Daniel;
- those chapters in the Gospels of Mark, Matthew and Luke to which scholars have given the general heading of 'Synoptic Apocalypse';
- the Revelation to John, that strange, difficult book which rounds off the canon of the New Testament.

That is why, in this reflection, I have focused primarily on those three areas of Scripture. I have also taken a sidelong glance at the letters of St Paul in the hope of untangling the alleged biblical bases for those teachings about 'The Rapture' which have gained such a hold over Evangelical Christians in the USA and in sub-Saharan Africa.

SIGNS OF THE TIMES

Introduction

In times when societies are stable and ordered, neither the Church nor the world finds a great deal of space for the apocalyptic writings of the Bible. They are left to those on the margins, socially, politically and theologically. In times of serious social, economic or political disturbance they tend to take a higher profile. It is in such times that the leaders of groups on the fringe tend to make predictions about 'the end of the age'.

However, to leave apocalyptic on one side until the media start using the word in their headlines is to ignore the serious social and political criticism which the apocalyptic writings contain. They remove the veil from societies and cultures in which exploitation and oppression are rife, albeit mainly hidden behind the facade of 'Classical civilization'. This may make them uncomfortable reading for comfortable churches, but that is in large measure their point. The letters to the seven churches of Asia in the opening chapters of Revelation aim their sharpest criticism at the communities which have become neither cold nor hot, like the church in Laodicea, or which have made too close an accommodation to the zeitgeist, while failing to listen to what the Spirit is saying to the churches.

In contemporary lectionaries the books of Daniel and Revelation often provide the readings at morning and evening prayer as the Church season approaches Advent. That is a context which reminds us that for many centuries the traditional themes of the weeks before Christmas were not focused on celebrating the first coming of Jesus Christ as the Child of Bethlehem but rather on his parousia, his 'second coming', to wind up human history and bring into being 'a new heaven and a new earth' (Rev. 21:1).

It is within this framework that Christians have studied those Biblical writings which set out the promise of Christ's coming and tried to understand what they have to say about 'the signs of the times'. The reflections in this book are intended to offer some guidance as we seek to interpret the signs of the times in this generation, an age of deep and growing uncertainty, change and anxiety. I hope, too, that they may play a part in recovering these writings for the wider Church rather than leaving them to fundamentalists and fringe sects. Mainstream Christians who ignore these books simply because of their exotic imagery and very different thought-world, are at risk of losing an important dimension of the faith which they profess.

Although the word 'apocalyptic' has become shorthand for 'unspeakably horrific and disastrous', it derives, like the word 'apocalypse', from the Greek verb ἀποκαλυπτεῖν (apokalyptein) which means 'to uncover' or 'to reveal'. Apocalyptic writings, then, purport to 'reveal' things that have been hidden by God from the earliest times until the day of the reader. They are usually written as if they come from the pen of someone who lived a very long time in the past, Enoch, or Seth, or Daniel. They are written as though they are a vision of the future, although the writer is, in fact, contemporary with the events that he is describing. They are also—and this is an important factor—written in a time of crisis which threatens to overwhelm God's people.

The Book of Daniel is most likely to have been written during the Maccabees' struggle against King Antiochus of Syria, when it appeared at one time as if the Jewish people and their sense of the unicity of God were about to be wiped off the face of the earth. It is generally thought that the book of Revelation was written in the face of a similar crisis for the Church in the time of the Emperor Domitian, who ruled AD 81–96.

Deciphering Daniel

The kind of writing that we call 'apocalyptic' originates in the Jewish thought-world that came into being after the people's return from exile in Babylon in the late sixth century BC. It has to be read in the light of Israel's history and of the prophets' proclamation of God's judgement against the moral, spiritual and political failures of God's people. The age of 'the latter prophets',[1] which stretches from Amos, Hosea and Isaiah of Jerusalem in the eighth century before Christ to Haggai, Zechariah and Malachi in the fifth, provides the soil and the seed out of which the exotic blossoms of apocalyptic writing can grow. Most of the books that scholars label 'apocalyptic' appeared in the time between the writing of the latest books of the Hebrew Scriptures and the composition of the earliest books of the Christian New Testament. But there are two books among the canon of the Hebrew Scriptures which contain examples of apocalyptic writing. They are the book of Daniel and, to a lesser extent, the later chapters of the prophecies of Zechariah.[2]

The book of Daniel is a product of the great crisis which overtook the Jewish people of Palestine in the first half of the second century BC. It is a curious book. In the Christian Bible, which follows the order of

---

[1] The Jewish designation covering the books of Isaiah, Jeremiah and Ezekiel and the twelve lesser prophets, as against 'the former prophets', which consist of the books of Joshua and Judges and the two books of Samuel and of Kings.

[2] The second half of the book (chapters 8–14) is sometimes described as 'Second Zechariah', by analogy with the traditional division of Isaiah's prophecies. The apocalyptic material comes mainly in chapters 12–14.

the Septuagint,³ it is numbered among the books of the prophets. In Article VII of the Thirty-nine Articles, one of the foundation documents of the Church of England, the Book of Daniel is counted among the 'four Prophets the greater' (the other three being Isaiah, Jeremiah, and Ezekiel). In the Jewish arrangement of their Scriptures, on the other hand, Daniel is to be found among 'The Writings', that group of books which belongs neither to 'The Law' nor to 'The Prophets' and which contains the Psalms, Proverbs, the Song of Solomon, Ecclesiastes, Esther, Job, Ruth, and Lamentations, as well as the two Books of Chronicles, and the memoirs of Ezra and Nehemiah.

The book of Daniel is curious, too, in another way. The first half is very different from the second in subject-matter, in style, and in the language in which it is written. From chapter two to chapter seven it is written in Aramaic, the language of everyday life across the Near East in the ancient world, and the story told in those six chapters is framed as a kind of historical novel—almost an adventure yarn of the kind printed in the *Boys' Own Paper* of my father's youth.

These opening chapters of the Book of Daniel are set fairly loosely in the time of King Nebuchadnezzar of Babylon and his successors. They tell the story of Daniel and his three friends, Hananiah, Mishael and Azariah, better known, perhaps, by the names, Shadrach, Meshach and Abednego, which were given to them by their Babylonian captors.⁴ These four young Jewish exiles are taken into royal service because of their outstanding personal qualities. At the king's court they are faced with various situations which test their loyalty to the God of Israel and their obedience to the Law of Moses. Each time, they pass the test with flying colours. They also prove themselves to be wiser and more courageous than all the astrologers, wizards, enchanters, sorcerers and wise men of the Babylonian kingdom. Daniel, in particular, is revealed as someone 'endowed with a

---

³ The translation of the Hebrew Bible into Greek which took place in Egypt under the patronage of king Ptolemy II (mid-third century BC).

⁴ Daniel is also given a Babylonian name, Belteshazzar (Dan. 1:7).

spirit of the holy gods' (Dan. 4:8f., 5:11), and each episode in the story ends with either a confession of the God of Israel as 'God of gods and Lord of kings' (Dan. 2:47) or a prohibition against speaking ill of the God worshipped by Daniel and his companions, the God who saves from the burning fiery furnace (Dan. 3:28–30) and from the lions' den (Dan. 6:25–8), the God by whose decree Nebuchadnezzar loses his kingdom and his reason, and becomes an outcast until 'seven times pass over him', because of the king's pride (Dan. 4:28–37), the God who who terrifies Belshazzar with the message of judgement written on the wall (Dan. 5:5–9, 13–28).

Then, in the second half of the book, everything changes. The language is no longer Aramaic, the lingua franca of the ancient Near East. From chapter 8 until the end of Chapter 12, the book of Daniel is written in Hebrew, the language of the learned and, perhaps more importantly, the devout among the Jewish people. With this change of language comes a change of style and a change of mood. Dreams and visions replace the adventure stories. Daniel becomes the sole human focus. The rulers of this world are no longer treated as essentially well-intentioned men who need to have their eyes opened to the reality of God's power and the limits of their own. Instead they are portrayed as beasts—aggressive and destructive monsters trampling and goring each other. The second half of Daniel, in a sense, represents a total rejection of what we might call 'the political process'. The rulers of this world have not only failed, they have become demonic.

Most scholars are agreed that the main reason for this change in perspective is the experience of the Jewish people during the reign of King Antiochus IV of Syria. Antiochus, whose reign lasted from 175 to 163 BC, ruled one of the kingdoms that the generals who had been Alexander the Great's comrades in arms had carved out of Alexander's empire after his death 150 years earlier. Like his predecessors, Antiochus saw it as part of his responsibility to ensure that Greek culture was firmly rooted in the lands and among the peoples that he governed. For Antiochus that included Palestine and its Jewish inhabitants.[5]

Some Jewish leaders had no problems with that. Jewish soldiers had, after all, fought with distinction alongside the Greeks in Alexander's armies and in the wars that followed his death. However, Antiochus's plans did not go down at all well among the population at large. Furthermore, Syrian attempts to impose cultural uniformity across the king's realm—which included setting up an image of the Greek god Zeus in the Temple on Mount Zion—were marked by heavy-handed brutality. This provoked an increasingly violent reaction, culminating in the uprising led by Judas Maccabaeus and his brothers. The books of the Maccabees, in the Apocrypha/Deuterocanonical writings, give something of the flavour of this struggle from the viewpoint of the Jewish resistance.

For Jews this was the greatest crisis since the capture of Jerusalem by Nebuchadnezzar 400 years earlier. Their faith, the faith that had sustained them through the pain of exile and in the difficult years following their return to Palestine, was again under sustained and brutal attack. Those observances which had enabled them to retain hold of their identity as the people of God—circumcision, the Sabbath, *kosher* food, rejection of idols—these were the primary target of the rulers and officials who sought to impose Greek culture across the region.

It might be tempting to see Antiochus as a kind of forerunner of Adolf Hitler. He was not. Greeks and non-Greeks shared alike in the benefits that flowed from Alexander's conquests and in the citizenship of the successor-states. There is no evidence for the kind of racist anti-Semitic ideology that inspired the Nazis' Final Solution. The

---

[5] The classic work on this period is probably still Martin Hengel, *Judaism and Hellenism: Studies in Their Encounter in Palestine During the Early Hellenistic Period* (Fortress Press, 1974). A more accessible account can be found in the same author's *Jews, Greeks and Barbarians: Aspects of the Hellenization of Judaism in the Pre-Christian Period* (Fortress Press, 1980).

struggle, from the king's point of view, was political and cultural, which meant inevitably, from the Jewish point of view, that it was religious. A closer parallel from our own time might be the treatment of the Muslim Uighurs of western China by the authorities in Beijing, or the forced conversions and martyrdoms among religious minorities in those parts of the Middle East which fell into the hands of Islamic State in the second decade of this century.

The significance of the book of Daniel in such a context is twofold. First, and positively, it reaffirms the sovereignty of God over history and over the rulers of this world. It reaffirms the importance of faithfulness to God's commandments. It is a book written to encourage a people preparing for martyrdom, strengthening their hope and confidence in the power of God to save — even in the kind of grim situation described by the books of the Maccabees. The beasts cannot win. Their power is given them for, at most, 'a time, two times and half a time' (Dan. 7:25, 12:7). That adds up to 3½, a number which in Jewish thought is associated with incompleteness. The attempt of the powers of this world to destroy the people of God will never come to fruition.

Second, and less positively, the book of Daniel can be seen as a kind of theological escapism. The Waldensian scholar Alberto Soggin described it as 'a flight from the historical reality in which the prophets lived so intensely, into metaphysics and myth'[6] and, as such, regressive. Another negative consequence has been the way in which the code used in the book of Daniel to describe situations and events in the mid-second century before Christ has been hi-jacked at various points in history by sectarian groups and made to fit their agendas. The symbols, the imagery and the use of numbers — which may appear strange and, perhaps, arbitrary to our eyes — are all carefully worked out and, as we shall see later, they convey a clear message to those who understand the conventions of ancient numerology. But among

---

[6] J. Alberto Soggin, *Introduction to the Old Testament: From Its Origins to the Closing of the Alexandrian Canon*, trans. John Bowden (rev. edn SCM Press, 1980), 412.

people who do not understand, or who ignore those conventions they have provided down the ages a basis for speculation and for wild and ultimately destructive messianic fantasies. They lie behind Mediaeval millennialist movements. They can be found in the German towns and cities in the sixteenth century which favoured the Radical Reformation, and in modern utopian communities such as those in Jonestown, Guyana, whose members perished by mass suicide in 1978, or in Waco, Texas, fifteen years later, where many lives were lost in the shoot-out between David Koresh's followers and the FBI.

There are, however, two elements in the book of Daniel which have left their mark on the development of Jewish and Christian thought for two millennia. One comes right at the end of the book, in chapter twelve. It is the first clear expression in Jewish writings of a doctrine of the resurrection of the dead at the end of time and it is found within the framework of an attempt to make sense of the sufferings of God's righteous servants:

> Many of those who sleep in the dust of the earth shall awake, some to everlasting life, and some to shame and everlasting contempt. Those who are wise shall shine like the brightness of the sky, and those who lead many to righteousness, like the stars forever and ever. ... But you, go your way, and rest; you shall rise for your reward at the end of the days. (Dan. 12:2–3, 13)

The other is to be found at the book's mid-point, where it pivots from historical romance to visionary denunciation. The language, like that of the preceding chapters, is still Aramaic, but the thought-world is that of the chapters which follow.

The seventh chapter of the book of Daniel begins with conflict between the beasts which represent the empires of Babylon, Media, Persia and Macedon. Then the scene shifts to the heavenly court in session before 'an Ancient One' (Dan. 7:9). There the beasts are condemned, and 'one like a human being' (or 'like a son of man' in older translations) is presented before the Ancient One to receive 'dominion and glory and kingship, that all peoples, nations, and languages should serve him' (Dan. 7:14). Here we have the one who represents God's suffering people and who, later in the chapter, is identified with 'the holy ones of the Most High' (Dan. 7:18) by the divine attendant whose task is to interpret the vision. For the writer of the book this is almost certainly Israel. But for two thousand years Christians have identified the 'one like a human being' with Jesus, who called himself 'Son of Man', and who took on himself the suffering, the sin and misery of the world.

Among Christians those words from the book of Daniel are often read at the Eucharist on Ascension Day, celebrating the exaltation of Jesus and the reception of his humanity, and ours, into the Godhead.[7] They remind us that the One who is given 'dominion, glory and kingship' overcomes the rulers of this world by submitting to their power to kill and destroy, taking his place, in every aspect of life from birth to death, among the outcast and despised, the oppressed, the humiliated, the marginalized. But they remind us, too, that beyond the death and the suffering—a suffering shared in the past century by countless millions of God's people: 'his dominion is an everlasting dominion that shall not pass away, and his kingship is one that shall never be destroyed' (Dan. 7:14). For Christians that indestructible kingship has been the goal toward which the signs of the times are pointing.

---

[7] Cf. Christopher Wordsworth's hymn, 'See, the Conqueror mounts in triumph' (NEW 132), especially verse 3:
>Thou hast raised our human nature
>In the clouds to God's right hand;
>There we sit in heavenly places,
>There with thee in glory stand;
>Jesus reigns, adored by angels;
>Man with God is on the throne;
>Mighty Lord, in thine Ascension
>We by faith behold our own.

GRAPPLING WITH THE GOSPELS

Albert Schweitzer in his classic study, *The Quest of the Historical Jesus* emphasized to liberal Protestants at the beginning of the twentieth century the important place of eschatology in the message of Jesus.[8] Their Christianity had become comfortably 'this-worldly' and Schweitzer, then barely into his thirties, was eager to offer a corrective. Much of the teaching of Jesus in the first three Gospels has to do with the nature of God's kingdom and with the imminence of its arrival. Jesus in his parables, like St Paul in his earlier letters, has a great deal to say about the coming of 'the day of the Lord'[9] or 'the Kingdom of God' and the importance of recognizing the signs of the times. Both Jesus and Paul taught that the coming of 'the Kingdom of God' was imminent, even that it was 'among you' or 'within you' (Luke 17:21). Jesus tells his disciples that 'this generation will not pass away until all things have taken place' (Luke 21:32) and encourages them to be alert to the signs of the times as a farmer is alert to the signs that indicate what the next day's weather will be (Matt. 16:3). Paul warns the Christian community in Thessalonica not to let an over-enthusiastic anticipation of the kingdom's coming get in the way of their everyday lives as Christian disciples (2 Thess. 3:6–15).[10] This, rather than a state-sponsored welfare programme, is the setting of the notorious text, 'Anyone unwilling to work should not eat' (2 Thess. 3:10).

---

[8] *Von Reimarus zu Wrede: Eine Geschichte der Leben-Jesu-Forschung* (J. C. B. Mohr, 1906): English translation with new introd. by William Montgomery as *The Quest of the Historical Jesus* (Macmillan, 1954).
[9] In the Gospels usually, and more elliptically, 'that day'.
[10] Compare also 1 Thessalonians 5:1–11 and 2 Thessalonians 2:1–11.

In the context of the letters to Thessalonica, it is appropriate to say something about the Rapture, a doctrine which has long rooted itself in the American Bible Belt and more recently among Christians in sub-Saharan Africa.[11] It also raised Jerry B. Jenkins and the late Tim LaHaye to the status of best-selling authors with the *Left Behind* multimedia franchise of apocalyptic fiction.[12]

The concept of the Rapture as popularly understood first appeared in England among Plymouth Brethren in the 1830s and became popular in the USA about eighty years later. It is a classic example of what is sometimes dismissed as 'concordance theology'. Those who espouse the concept take what Jesus has to say in Matthew 24 and Luke 17 about two people working, or sleeping, in the same place and one of them being taken and the other left (Matt. 24:40–1, Luke 17:34–5), and set those sayings alongside a passage in St Paul's first letter to the Thessalonians, where Paul writes to encourage believers who are mourning fellow-Christians who have died before the anticipated coming of Christ in glory.

> We do not want you to be uninformed, brothers and sisters, about those who have died, so that you may not grieve as others do who have no hope. For since we believe that Jesus died and rose again, even so, through Jesus, God will bring with him those who have died. For this we declare to you by the word of the Lord, that we who are alive, who are left until the coming of the Lord, will by no means precede those who have died. For the Lord himself, with a cry of command, with the archangel's call and with the sound of God's trumpet, will descend from heaven, and the dead in Christ will rise first. Then we who are alive, who are left, will be caught up in the clouds together with them to meet the Lord in the air; and so

---

[11] It is reportedly so beloved of American fundamentalists that there is a market for car bumper stickers printed with the words 'In the event of the Rapture this automobile will become unmanned'.

[12] The sixteen novels published between 1995 and 2007, were adapted into five films; there is also an audio drama and a computer game spin-off from the original novels.

we will be with the Lord for ever. Therefore encourage one another with these words. (1 Thess. 4:13–18)

From these two entirely disparate elements they create a scenario in which—just before the time of tribulation, the 'birth pangs', to which Jesus refers as preceding the final coming of the Son of Man (Matt. 24:8, Mark 13:8)—those who are true believers will be removed to safety in heaven while those who are not will endure suffering and disaster on earth.

That fantasy may sell books and seats in the cinema, but it is based on a serious misreading of Scripture and a failure to put either Jesus's words or Paul's into their proper context. The words of Jesus would have summoned up for his first-century hearers a picture of the Roman army's practice, similar to that of the naval press-gang in eighteenth-century England, of seizing members of subject peoples and marching them away to undertake forced labour. It is therefore those who are taken who are about to experience a time of tribulation, rather than those who are left behind. This imagery, moreover, is totally unrelated to the thinking which lies behind St Paul's words in 1 Thessalonians 4: there Paul takes as his starting-point not the descent of the press-gang on an unsuspecting community, but an official visit to a city by an emperor, king, or provincial governor. As the official cortège approached, the leading citizens would go out to meet it and escort the emperor and his entourage into the city with great pomp and ceremony. Paul's point is that both the living and the resurrected dead will be part of that escort when Christ comes in glory, 'caught up in the clouds...to meet the Lord in the air' (1 Thess. 4:17), so that together they may accompany him back to earth when he comes as ruler and judge of all.[13] They are not crowding into a cosmic escape pod which will take them out of earthly danger into the safety of heaven!

---

[13] Karen Armstrong, *St Paul The Misunderstood Apostle* (Atlantic Books, 2015), 67. See also Nicholas T. Wright, *Paul: In Fresh Perspective* (Fortress Press, 2005), 55–6.

Careful readers of what Jesus has to say about the end of the age will realize two things in particular:[14] first, that Jesus warns his hearers that the day and the hour cannot be predicted:

> About that day and hour no one knows, neither the angels of heaven, nor the Son, but only the Father. (Matt. 24:36)

Second, that sharing in suffering is an all-but-inevitable consequence of the call to follow Jesus. Before the end comes, those who have responded to that call must be prepared for a world in turmoil, where conflict, natural disasters, epidemics, and dissension and betrayal even among their nearest and dearest are the norm.

> As for yourselves, beware; for they will hand you over to councils; and you will be beaten in synagogues; and you will stand before governors and kings because of me, as a testimony to them. And the good news must first be proclaimed to all nations. When they bring you to trial and hand you over, do not worry beforehand about what you are to say; but say whatever is given you at that time, for it is not you who speak, but the Holy Spirit. Brother will betray brother to death, and a father his child, and children will rise against parents and have them put to death; and you will be hated by all because of my name. But the one who endures to the end will be saved.
> But when you see the desolating sacrilege set up where it ought not to be (let the reader understand), then those in Judea must flee to the mountains... (Mark 13:9–14)[15]

They are not, however, to imagine for a moment that 'this is it'. Jesus warns his disciples that, 'This is but the beginning of the birth pangs' (Matt. 13:8).

That choice of words is significant. Readers of the Synoptic Apocalypse, and of the more elaborate texts in Daniel and Revelation, often treat it as though it is about The End. The words of Jesus, on the other hand, remind us that what is being revealed is a new beginning,

---

[14] Principally in Mark 13, in Matthew 24, and in chapters 17 and 21 of Luke's gospel.
[15] Cf. Matt. 24:9–16, Luke 21:12–21.

the opening of a new age which will be inaugurated by the coming of the Son of Man (Mark 13:26–7 and parallels), and therefore a birth even though it may seem like a kind of death. This has a secular counterpart, perhaps, in the way in which many environmental scientists, pondering the impending end of the Anthropocene Era, make the point that in all likelihood life on earth will go on in some way, however dire the forecasts of ecological disaster may be. Life will go on, even if human beings are not part of the new age inaugurated by the end of human domination of the planet—or if they survive, but are stripped of the dominant role in relation to other creatures which they have previously enjoyed.

In some respects the Synoptic Apocalypse reprises the pattern of the second half of Daniel, with echoes of its language, and occasionally direct quotation, most obviously the reference to 'an abomination that desolates' at Matthew 24:15, Mark 13:14.[16] What it lacks is the roll-call of fabulous monsters which appears in Daniel 7 and 8. The words of Jesus which the Gospels record are low-key and matter-of-fact by comparison and the content of his warnings reflects the realities of life in Roman-occupied Palestine, and especially the events surrounding the first Roman-Jewish War of AD 66–73.[17] Even the various references to geological and meteorological or astronomical disturbance (Mark 13:7–8, 24–5 and parallels) reflect the preoccupations of a culture which held that 'when beggars die there are no comets seen; The heavens themselves blaze forth the death of princes',[18] rather than cosmic conflict with the forces of personified evil. In the place of Daniel's vivid descriptions of supernatural beasts, there are warnings of disturbance to the natural order of things and of political upheavals. There are also repeated cautions against false prophets and false messiahs

---

[16] Quoting Dan. 9:27.
[17] See, for example, Ched Myers, *Binding the Strong Man: A Political Reading of Mark's Story of Jesus* (Orbis, 1988), 324–48.
[18] Shakespeare, *Julius Caesar*, II.ii.

who seek to lead believers astray (Mark 13:5f, 21f; Luke 21:7f), and repeated encouragements to keep awake and alert to the signs of the times.

> But about that day and hour no one knows, neither the angels of heaven, nor the Son, but only the Father. For as the days of Noah were, so will be the coming of the Son of Man. For as in those days before the flood they were eating and drinking, marrying and giving in marriage, until the day Noah entered the ark, and they knew nothing until the flood came and swept them all away, so too will be the coming of the Son of Man. Then two will be in the field; one will be taken and one will be left. Two women will be grinding meal together; one will be taken and one will be left. Keep awake therefore, for you do not know on what day your Lord is coming. But understand this: if the owner of the house had known in what part of the night the thief was coming, he would have stayed awake and would not have let his house be broken into. Therefore you also must be ready, for the Son of Man is coming at an unexpected hour.
> (Matt. 24:36–44)

Those signs of the times, in Luke's account, include a detailed forecast of the destruction of Jerusalem and the deportation of its inhabitants 'until the times of the Gentiles are fulfilled' (Luke 21:20–4). Such predictions are sufficiently close to other writers' descriptions of what happened to Jerusalem during the later stages of the first Roman-Jewish war to suggest that Luke may have written his Gospel after that war's end.[19] The detailed description, and Jesus's repeated warnings to flee, are sandwiched between prophecies of turmoil and persecution on the one hand (Luke 21:8–17) and the cosmic disturbances which precede 'the Son of Man coming in a cloud' on the other (Luke 21:25–8), picking up the imagery of Daniel 7 and being picked up at a later point in the Passion narrative during Jesus's interrogation before the Sanhedrin.

---

[19] See, for example, Josephus, *De Bello Judaico*, Book VI, and Tacitus, *Histories*, Book V.

> They [the members of the Sanhedrin] said, 'If you are the Messiah, tell us.' He replied, 'If I tell you, you will not believe; and if I question you, you will not answer. But from now on the Son of Man will be seated at the right hand of the power of God.' (Luke 22:67–9)[20]

By way of a footnote to this brief discussion of the Synoptic Apocalypse: I remember an earnest conversation fifty years ago with a couple of friends at university, as we tried to work out whether it would be preferable to live through the last days and see Christ's coming in glory or to die before the times of tribulation arrived and cut straight to the resurrection. Unfortunately, I cannot remember what conclusion our discussion reached. I suspect that we remained undecided. Neither prospect, as I recall, appealed greatly to a trio of young men in their early twenties. Jesus, however, is clear about one thing: 'The one who endures to the end will be saved' (Matt. 10:22, Mark 13:13, cf. Luke 21:19).

That '[enduring] to the end' is part of our reaction to the signs of the times and, in particular, our response to the promise of Christ's coming. As Albert Schweitzer wrote at the end of his epic quest,

> He comes to us as One unknown, without a name, as of old, by the lake-side, He came to those men who knew him not. He speaks to us the same word: 'Follow thou me' and sets us to the task which He has to fulfil for our time. He commands. And to those who obey Him, whether they be wise or simple, He will reveal Himself in the toils, the conflicts, the sufferings which they shall pass through in His fellowship, and as an ineffable mystery, they shall learn in their own experience Who He is.[21]

---

[20] Luke's echo is a paler reflection of Mark's direct quotation of this passage:
>   Again the high priest asked him, 'Are you the Messiah, the Son of
>   the Blessed One?' Jesus said, 'I am and
>   'you will see the Son of Man
>   seated at the right hand of the Power',
>   and 'coming with the clouds of heaven.' (Mark 14:61–2).

[21] Schweitzer, *The Quest of the Historical Jesus*, 401.

A Reading of Revelation

For many mainstream Christians the memory of doorstep encounters with Jehovah's Witnesses or members of other sects has given the Revelation to John a bad name. It is a book that is open to misuse and misunderstanding. And it is disturbing. It seems, somehow, to plug effortlessly into the worst nightmares of humankind. Even in this allegedly scientific age, our worst fears find their place among John's twenty-two chapters. Economic meltdown, environmental degradation, military disaster, prisoners of conscience, power worship, ideological enslavement to false gods and false prophets — all are there. Perhaps it is no wonder that this book was one of the last to find acceptance in the canon of the New Testament. Even then doubts have continued, from the Reformation to the present day. Martin Luther claimed that 'his spirit could not put up with this book'.[22] The great twentieth-century New Testament scholar Rudolf Bultmann described the content of Revelation as 'a weakly Christianized Judaism'.[23]

In most places it was accepted into the Christian canon of Scripture on the basis of its supposed authorship by John son of Zebedee, also generally assumed to be the John who wrote the fourth Gospel. But that authorship was questioned as early as the third century, when Bishop Dionysius of Alexandria pointed out the wide differences in style, language and thought between Revelation and

---

[22] Quoted in Werner G. Kümmel, *Introduction to the New Testament* (Abingdon Press, 1975), 473. Kümmel continues that for Luther 'Revelation was too much concerned with tales and pictures and in it Christ was neither taught nor made known.'

[23] Rudolf Bultmann, *Theology of the New Testament*, 175. Cited in Kümmel, *Introduction to the New Testament*, 473.

the other writings from John or his circle.[24] Revelation appears to have been written by someone whose first language was not Greek but Aramaic.[25] It is full of ideas and images taken from the Hebrew Scriptures. Indeed it is steeped in them, especially in the writings of the prophets. Although John hardly ever quotes directly from the Hebrew Scriptures, echoes of or allusions to Isaiah, Daniel, Amos, Ezekiel (especially), and Zechariah are referenced in the margin of many study Bibles, as are the Psalms, and the books of the Law.

That offers a clue about how to read Revelation. We need to set it firmly within the framework of a first-century Jewish thought-world. We need to see it in the light of the prophets' proclamation of God's judgement against his sinful people and in the light of those other writings from the years 'between the Testaments' in which the Book of Daniel took shape.

However, John's book is different from those older books in a number of significant respects. He does not try to hide behind the name of some great figure from the past.[26] He writes simply as 'John', and tells us he was an exile on the island of Patmos. Whoever he was, he was clearly well known to the Christian communities of Asia[27] and, equally clearly, recognized as having authority among them. It is clear, too, from the local details in the letters to the Seven Churches which take the book on from John's initial vision that, despite his exile, he knew well the communities to which he was writing.

In works that come from a Jewish background, symbols and images work on the ear rather than the eye. Much of the effectiveness of

---

[24] John Sweet, *Revelation*, SCM Pelican Commentaries (SCM Press, 1979), 36f.

[25] Kümmel quotes with approval J. Schmid's comment in *Theologische Revue*, 62 (1966), 306, that the author of Revelation 'thought in Hebrew but wrote in Greek', *Introduction to the New Testament*, 465.

[26] The suggestion that the book was attributed to John son of Zebedee pseudonymously can be ruled out for a number of reasons. See Sweet, *Revelation*, 37–8.

[27] Viz. the Roman province, which consisted of western Asia Minor, modern Turkey's Aegean coastal region.

Hebrew prophecy depends on word-play and puns. We might remember Amos and his basket of summer fruit (Amos 8:1–2),[28] or Jeremiah and his branch of almond (Jer. 1:11f)[29] — and the children of Isaiah and Hosea with their highly symbolic names.[30]

In the same way, John's images tend to be verbal rather than visual. There is a fourteenth-century tapestry in the château at Angers which is one of the wonders of the mediaeval world and which unintentionally makes that point. It treats the whole book of Revelation as a mediaeval cartoon strip — which just shows how long the *bande dessinée* has been regarded in France as an art form — and it shows very clearly how difficult it is to reproduce in visual form some of the figures which John 'sees'; even such an apparently straightforward image as the figure of Christ among the lamp standards at the beginning of the book.

> I saw seven golden lampstands, and in the midst of the lampstands I saw one like the Son of Man, clothed with a long robe and with a golden sash across his chest. His head and his hair were white as white wool, white as snow; his eyes were like a flame of fire, his feet were like burnished bronze, refined as in a furnace, and his voice was like the sound of many waters. In his right hand he held seven stars, and from his mouth came a sharp, two-edged sword, and his face was like the sun shining with full force. (Rev. 1:12–16)

That description is full of very powerful symbols drawn from the rich stock provided by the Hebrew Scriptures. But when the attempt is made to represent them in visual form they can appear bizarre, if not downright silly. The idea of God's word as a sharp, two-edged

---

[28] The play in Amos is on the Hebrew words *qayits* (= summer fruit) and *qets* (= end).

[29] The Jeremiah passage depends on the similarity between *shaqed* (= almond) and *shoqed* (= watching).

[30] Isaiah's son was named Maher-shalal-hash-baz (Is. 8:1–3), meaning 'The spoil speeds, the prey hastens.' Hosea's children (Hos. 1:4–9) were Jezreel (God sows), Lo-ruhamah (Not pitied) and Lo-ammi (Not my people).

sword is a powerful one and occurs elsewhere in the Bible.[31] But if that verbal image is turned into a visual one it looks very strange. That is, perhaps, a useful warning against trying to interpret this book literally. John did not expect his original readers to take everything he wrote at face value; he expected them to look for a deeper meaning. That is clear from the invitation, 'Let anyone who has an ear listen to what the Spirit is saying to the Churches.' Those words are repeated at the end of each of the seven letters (Rev. 2:7, 11, 17, 29; 3:6, 13, 22).

'Let them listen'. That is another clue to interpreting the meaning of Revelation. Repeatedly, John hears one of the supernatural beings say or do something which is then interpreted by the vision that he sees. For example, in chapter 7 John *hears* the number of the servants of God, 'a hundred and forty-four thousand sealed, out of every tribe of the people of Israel' (Rev. 7:4–8). He then *sees* 'a great multitude which no man could number, from every nation, from all tribes and peoples and tongues' (Rev. 7:9). The counting of the 144,000, the perfect reality of God's people which John *hears,* is the theological truth. The countless multitude which he *sees* is the outward reality of a salvation promised to all nations. These are not two different groups but one group understood in two ways: from the point of view of human experience and from the point of view of God's eternal purpose.

That figure of 144,000 is a reminder that numbers were important in the world in which John lived. They were important not simply for denoting quantity, but because for many people they had symbolic meaning. Traces of that survive to the present day in popular superstitions about numbers being 'lucky' or 'unlucky'. In the ancient world such numerological schemes were much more fully worked out.

Here, again, is an argument against taking John's writing at face value, without thinking about the deeper meaning that would have been conveyed to his original readers. That meaning is not necessarily simple—any more than John's use of symbols generally is simple. As well as carrying some fairly straightforward meanings, they may refer

---

[31] Hebrews 4:12. Cf. Ephesians 6:17.

back to a specific passage in the Old Testament.[32] So, the recurring period of 3½ years, expressed in terms of days or months (Rev. 11:2f, 12:6, 13:5), may refer back to Daniel's use of the mysterious 'a time, two times and half a time' (Dan. 7.25, 12:7) that I mentioned above, as the period left before his vision comes to be. It seems, in general, to signify incompleteness or limitation.[33]

Nor is it only numbers which have hidden meanings. John combines and re-arranges ideas from a variety of sources. His picture of heaven, for example, draws on the temple, the synagogue, the theatre and the imperial games, and the symbols do not necessarily have a single layer of meaning. The twenty-four elders seated around the throne (Rev. 4:4) may refer to the twenty-four heads of priestly families listed in 1 Chronicles 24:4–6. They may equally be the twelve patriarchs of Israel, who give their names to the twelve gates of the heavenly city, and the twelve apostles of the Lamb, whose names are written on its foundations (Rev. 21:12–14). The sea of glass in front of God's throne may look back to Solomon's temple (2 Chron. 3–5). It may reflect Jewish traditions about a heavenly parallel to the Red Sea. It may even represent the final taming of the sea as against the great swirling abyss of chaos, the *tohu w'bohu* with which the book of Genesis begins (Gen. 1:2).

The place-names also carry a lot of symbolic weight—as Guernica or Hiroshima, for example, might do for us. When John writes about Sodom, Egypt, Babylon or Jerusalem, his readers would pick up layer upon layer of meaning which the Old Testament had given to those names: Sodom, the place of arrogance, wickedness and inhospitality; Egypt, the place of slavery; Babylon, the place of exile; Jerusalem, the ambiguous centre of the Jewish world and God's special place.

---

[32] 12, for instance, being the number of Israel and 7 the number of completion (see Sweet, *Revelation*, 14–15 for more examples).

[33] The number 3½ also counts the days during which the inhabitants of the earth are permitted to gloat over the death of the two witnesses (Rev. 11:9–12: cf. Sweet, *Revelation*, 182–3).

Another important clue to the understanding of Revelation is to look at it in the light of Jesus's own teaching about the last days, the 'Synoptic Apocalypse' which was considered in the previous chapter. Some scholars have seen Revelation as an up-date of that teaching in the light of the events that followed the destruction of Jerusalem in AD 70. History had moved on, the kingdom had not come, and the people of God needed reassurance that God was still at work in this new situation.

It is worth noting that John does not set out his story in a strictly chronological order. He picks up themes from one part of the book and weaves them into a later section.[34] This warns us to beware of those who think that they can turn the book into a sort of detailed long-range forecast and calendar of the End Time. John's concern is with the here-and-now, and at the time when John was writing the here-and-now included the Roman emperor Domitian (AD 51–96). He was the first emperor to be styled 'Lord and God' in his own lifetime.[35] His predecessors had all been happy to wait for divine honours until after their deaths,[36] but Domitian claimed the worship as well as the loyalty of his subjects while he was alive. It seems clear that Revelation is a Christian counter to imperial propaganda and to an overweening ruler who saw the state as his personal plaything, much as Daniel, two centuries earlier, had been a counter-blast against what were, in Jewish eyes, the blasphemous pretensions of Antiochus IV, who had added *Epiphanes* ('Manifest God') to his other royal titles.

---

[34] Austin Farrer's commentary on Revelation, *The Revelation of St John the Divine* (Clarendon Press, 1964) and his earlier study *A Rebirth of Images: the making of St John's Apocalypse* (Dacre Press, 1949) take great trouble in working out these relationships, sometimes perhaps over-elaborately.

[35] Suetonius, *Domitian*, 13.2.; Dio Cassius, *Histories*, 67.4.7.

[36] Domitian's father, the emperor Vespasian, is said to have joked on his deathbed about his impending deification. Suetonius reports his last words as *Væ, ut puto, deus fio!* ('Oh dear! I think I'm becoming a god!') Suetonius, *Vespasian*, 23.4

Revelation has been characterized as the most political book in the New Testament, both in its original points of reference and in later interpretation.[37] Certainly it provides an interpretation of the Roman Empire which is very different from the official version put out by the historians and poets of the early Caesars. This, as Elisabeth Schüssler Fiorenza points out in her commentary on Revelation, is what makes the book popular with 'disadvantaged and alienated minority groups', whether 'Bible-believing' Christians in the poor rural areas of the USA or oppressed and disadvantaged Christians in Latin America and southern Africa.[38]

This is one factor that makes Revelation more than simply a tract for its own times. It speaks for the 'Church from below'[39] in every age and every place, for the marginalized and dispossessed who joined in millenarian movements in the Middle Ages or who flocked to the banners of the radical Reformation, and for revolutionary utopian movements in our own day. These are people for whom the world as it is, far from being a comfortable place, is as monstrous as the Hellenistic world of Antiochus appeared to devout Jews in the time of the Maccabees. This also goes some way to explaining the suspicion with which established and more hierarchical Churches handle it. There is, for example, no place for it in the lectionary of the Greek Orthodox Church.[40] In a text in which political power is seen, as in

---

[37] See, for example Elisabeth Schüssler Fiorenza and John Sweet in the introduction to their respective commentaries (Schüssler Fiorenza, *Revelation: Vision of a Just World* (T. & T. Clark, 1993), 1–33, especially 6–20; Sweet, *Revelation*, 1–52, especially 1–4, 27–35). Compare also the summary given in Kümmel, *Introduction to the New Testament*, 458–62 and Raymond E. Brown, *An Introduction to the New Testament*, (Doubleday, 1997), 800–2.

[38] Schüssler Fiorenza, *Revelation*, 7.

[39] A self-description originating among the members of the Christian resistance against Hitler and their post-war successors in West and (particularly) East Germany.

[40] Schüssler Fiorenza, *Revelation*, 6.

Daniel's day, as a devouring monster which crushes all before it (Rev. 13:4ff), and in which global commerce is depicted as

> the great whore... with whom the kings of the earth have committed fornication, and with the wine of whose fornication the inhabitants of the earth have become drunk. (Rev. 17:1f)[41]

locked in an ultimately-destructive relationship with the beast and the ten kings (Rev. 17:16–18), there is little space for the advocates of pragmatic, liberal compromise.

Indeed there are times and places where such compromise is not appropriate, or indeed possible. During the past century we have seen leaders and states which have claimed a status for themselves which is not compatible with the Christian and Jewish insistence that there is one God, the maker of heaven and earth and all that is in them, and that God alone is Lord. John holds out for the truth of the Christian claim. He makes it clear that there are areas—not only with regard to Church-state relations—where it is not possible to compromise with the spirit of the age, even if that resistance means martyrdom. There are some truths that it is worth suffering and, if need be, dying for, as Christ himself suffered and died... and conquered. That is the message of the letters. It is the message of the seals and the trumpets and the bowls. It is a message of warning and of encouragement from a pastor to the congregations that made up his flock.

In reading some of the more spectacular passages of Revelation, it is important that we understand that much of what John is saying about the evils and the plagues is not threatening God's judgement so much as describing the world in which John lives. They are, so to speak, the 'facts of life' about the first century of our era—and, we are coming increasingly to realize, about our own century, too. Those Four Horsemen of the Apocalypse, War, Famine, Disease and Death (Rev. 6:1–8), were a reality for John and for the people for whom he was writing, just as they have been for millions of people during

---

[41] Cf. the weeping merchants and seafarers in Rev. 18.

much of the last 150 years and as they are in many parts of the world today, where pandemic and climate crisis are exacerbating existing conflicts and the consequent movements of people. The famous *Pax Romana* did not preclude the possibility of disasters. In the second half of the first century the Roman empire experienced military defeats, volcanic eruptions, fire, plague and famines. This was the world which John knew and in which, despite everything, he proclaimed the ultimate victory of God and his Messiah.

One of the charges against John is that in places his language comes across as vindictive.[42] In some passages this is certainly the case, but it is important to recognize that running through the whole of the book there is a thread which deals with trial and judgement. Christians are being put on trial and condemned by earthly courts. The repeated prayers for vindication (e.g. Rev. 6:9–11) are a plea for the supreme court of heaven to put the record straight. It is a demand not for private vengeance but for public justice, justice that is not only done but seen to be done.[43] This is certainly true of the description of the fall of Babylon in chapter 18. The harshest language there is reserved for the supernatural powers of evil, and not for human beings. Babylon is not simply Rome; Babylon is 'the wicked city', a description which has been applied in books, and on stage and screen, to many cities from Los Angeles to Hong Kong via Atlanta, Marseille and Melbourne. Babylon is John Bunyan's *Vanity Fair* in all its pomp.

---

[42] This accusation has been made by authors as different in time and temperament as the eighteenth-century German biblical scholar, Johann Salomo Semler, *Abhandlung von freier Untersuchung des Canon*, 4 vols. (Gütersloher Verlagshaus Gerd Mohn, 1771–1773), vol. i, 75 (cited in Werner G. Kümmel, *The New Testament: The History of the Investigation of its Problems* (Abingdon Press, 1972), 63), the Swiss psychologist Carl Jung, *Answer to Job*, trans. Richard F. Carrington Hull (Routledge & Kegan Paul, 1954), 121–34 (cited in Sweet, *Revelation*, 43) and the English writer D. H. Lawrence, *Apocalypse* (Heinemann, 1931), 32–3, (cited in Sweet, *Revelation*, 48–51).

[43] Hans-Ruedi Weber, *The Way of the Lamb: Christ in the Apocalypse* (WCC Publications, 1988), 29.

It is also true that, at least in the earlier part of the book, the punishments are intended to lead to repentance. They are a call to human beings to change their ways and their outlook before it is too late. Other punishments are intended to bring home the consequences of worshipping evil and not God. Here again, the harshest language is reserved for the supernatural powers rather than their human agents. One might find points of comparison with the message of environmental campaigners. It is not difficult to read John's vision of the seven seals (Rev. 6), the seven trumpets (Rev. 8) and the seven bowls (Rev. 16) as foreshadowing the environmental catastrophe which human greed and short-sightedness are inflicting on the earth in our own age. It is unnerving to realize that the reaction of the greedy and short-sighted humans whose consumption has contributed to that catastrophe—us, in other words—is not significantly different from John's description of the human reaction to the pouring out of the seven bowls of God's wrath in Revelation 16. Despite the increasingly visible consequences of climate change, people who can afford to use aircraft in order to travel to destinations which are accessible by rail, still do so.[44] Governments still privilege the use of the motor-car over the means of public transport when deciding their spending priorities and, encouraged by the international financial system, hand out licences to those who wish to exploit the earth's remaining reserves of fossil fuels. Sea cruises remain a popular form of holiday-making. Massive container ships glide between the world's ports. Both release massive amounts of carbon into the earth's atmosphere. People who, in their private lives, are caring and responsible, both as family members and citizens, appear to lose sight of their need to care and to be responsible in their working environment. They have become Reinhold Niebuhr's 'moral man and immoral society' made flesh for the twenty-first century.[45]

---

[44] I include myself under this condemnation.
[45] Reinhold Niebuhr, *Moral Man and Immoral Society: A Study in Ethics and Politics* (C. Scribner's Sons, 1932).

To sum up: Revelation was written by a pastor to encourage and warn his flock in a particular situation of crisis. It is not a work of systematic theology. But there are themes and perspectives which can help us to assess what John is saying.

For every condemnation of supernatural wickedness there is an affirmation of the openness of the heavenly city and of the temple. At the very least it seems to be the case that at the time when John was writing he regarded the Book of Life as still being open.[46] The letters to the seven churches of Asia all represent a call to amendment of life, rather than the handing down of a final judgement. The outlook of the final chapters is cosmic and positive.

This puts Revelation in line with the rest of the New Testament: despite the strangeness of its imagery and expression it is not out on a theological limb. Its vision of the end of the world as it is chimes in with the teaching of Jesus, and its view of salvation as past, achieved in the sacrifice of the Lamb; present, in the work of the Spirit in the Churches; and future, when God brings about a new heaven and a new earth, is one that is reflected elsewhere in the New Testament. It shares the conviction of the Gospels that the Second Coming, the *parousia*, of Jesus is not subject to human calculation (Matt. 24:36). It shares Paul's view that 'you reap whatever you sow' (Gal. 6:7f), and its understanding of the wrath of God has a lot in common with Paul's account of the wrath as an impersonal force like the Eastern concept of karma.

In addition, Revelation identifies God and Jesus very closely. The expression 'God and the Lamb' is used many times. Worship is offered to both. Indeed, the foundation and governing concept of the entire book is the self-sacrificing, suffering Lamb, the present and future Christ, who is, in the words of one New Testament scholar, 'of central significance for the total view of divine history and for the present situation of the Christian community'.[47]

---

[46] Cf. Sweet, *Revelation*, 212.
[47] Kümmel, *Introduction to the New Testament*, 474.

One final point: all the judgmental language in Revelation is to be found in the middle of the book, as the struggle between the forces of God and the forces of evil represented by the dragon and the beasts is played out. The positive message comes at the beginning and the end—in Jewish thought the most significant positions. And the beginning and the end of Revelation, like the teaching of Jesus and the letters of Paul, are about hope, and endurance, and the fulfilment of the signs of the times in Christ's coming to renew and make whole.

Postscript

In this book I have attempted to uncover what the apocalyptic writings were aiming to reveal about God's action in the world in the age when they were composed. I hope that it may also encourage contemporary readers to think how their message might be interpreted for people of faith in the present age, which is facing threats at least as serious as those which seemed about to overwhelm believers, whether Jewish or Christian, during the two centuries of conflict and continuing crisis which stretched from the age of Antiochus IV Epiphanes (c. 215–164 BC) to that of the Flavian Caesars from AD 69 to 96.

What is important is the message of hope which accompanies the proclamation of Divine Judgement. That hope was embodied for Daniel in the 'one like a Son of Man/Human One' (Dan. 7:13); the one whom Christians, probably following Jesus himself, identified with their Lord.[48] Jesus, as we have seen, repeatedly urges his disciples to be alert to the signs of the times and to endure steadfastly whatever disasters and betrayals those times may bring. Finally, John the Seer reaffirms Daniel's message of judgement on the nations while emphasizing the glory and universal authority of Christ, the 'Lamb standing as if it had been slaughtered' (Rev. 5:6). The Lamb alone is found worthy to open the scroll sealed with seven seals which sets in motion the beginning of the birth-pangs and it is in the Lamb's marriage-feast that the whole of human history is consummated and the whole of creation transformed. In John's vision, the fulfilment to which the signs of the times point is finally realized in the 'new heaven and new

---

[48] Myers, *Binding the Strong Man*, 122–3.

earth' focused on the heavenly Jerusalem which is the dwelling-place of God and the Lamb, perpetually open to all the nations and eternally illuminated by the light of Christ.

> I saw no temple in the city, for its temple is the Lord God the Almighty and the Lamb. And the city has no need of sun or moon to shine on it, for the glory of God is its light, and its lamp is the Lamb. The nations will walk by its light, and the kings of the earth will bring their glory into it. Its gates will never be shut by day—and there will be no night there. People will bring into it the glory and the honour of the nations. (Rev. 21:22–6)

Suggested Further Reading

1. On Apocalyptic generally:

Brueggemann, Walter, *Introduction to the Old Testament* (Presbyterian Publishing Corporation, 2003).

Kümmel, W. G. *Introduction to the New Testament* (rev. edn Abingdon Press, 1975).

Lawrence, D. H., *Apocalypse* (Heinemann, 1931).

Russell, David S. *Between the Testaments* (SCM Press, 1960).

——, *The Method and Message of Jewish Apocalyptic: 200 BC – AD 100* (SCM Press, 1964).

——, *Divine Disclosure: An Introduction to Jewish Apocalyptic* (SCM Press, 1992).

Soggin, J. Alberto, *Introduction to the Old Testament: From Its Origins to the Closing of the Alexandrian Canon*, trans. John Bowden (rev. English edn, SCM Press, 1980).

Brian McLaren, *Life after Doom: Wisdom and Courage for a World Falling Apart* (Hodder & Stoughton, 2024).

2. On Daniel and the second-century background:

Porteous, Norman, *Daniel* (London, 1979).

Hengel, Martin, *Judaism and Hellenism: Studies in Their Encounter in Palestine During the Early Hellenistic Period* (Fortress Press, 1974).

——, *Jews, Greeks and Barbarians: Aspects of the Hellenization of Judaism in the Pre-Christian Period* (Fortress Press, 1980).

Brueggemann, Walter, *God, Neighbour, Empire* (SCM Press, 2017).

(and the relevant chapters in the works by Brueggemann and Soggin cited in 1. above)

3. On Paul

Armstrong, Karen, *St Paul The Misunderstood Apostle* (Atlantic Books, 2015).

Wright, Nicholas T., *Paul: In Fresh Perspective* (Fortress Press, 2005).

4. On the Gospels

Evans, Christopher F., *Saint Luke* (SCM Press, 1990).

Fenton, John, *Saint Matthew* (Penguin, 1963).

Hooker, Morna D., *The Message of Mark* (Epworth Press, 1983).

Myers, Ched, *Binding the Strong Man: A Political Reading of Mark's Story of Jesus* (Orbis, 1988).

5. On Revelation

Farrer, Austin, *A Rebirth of Images: the making of St John's Apocalypse* (Dacre Press, 1949).

———, *The Revelation of St John the Divine* (Clarendon Press, 1964).

Schüssler Fiorenza, Elisabeth, *Revelation: Vision of a Just World* (T. & T. Clark, 1993).

Sweet, John, *Revelation* SCM Pelican Commentaries (SCM Press, 1979).

Weber, Hans-Ruedi, *The Way of the Lamb: Christ in the Apocalypse* (WCC Publications, 1988).

SLG PRESS PUBLICATIONS

FP1	*Prayer and the Life of Reconciliation*	Gilbert Shaw (1969)
FP2	*Aloneness not Loneliness*	Mother Mary Clare SLG (1969)
FP4	*Intercession*	Mother Mary Clare SLG (1969)
FP8	*Prayer: Extracts from the Teaching of Father Gilbert Shaw*	Gilbert Shaw (1973)
FP12	*Learning to Pray*	Mother Mary Clare SLG (1970, rev. 3/2025)
FP15	*Death, the Gateway to Life*	Gilbert Shaw (1971, 3/2024)
FP16	*The Victory of the Cross*	Dumitru Stăniloae (1970, 3/2023)
FP26	*The Message of Saint Seraphim*	Irina Gorainov (1974)
FP28	*Julian of Norwich: Four Studies to Commemorate the Sixth Centenary of the Revelations of Divine Love*	Sister Benedicta Ward SLG, Sister Eileen Mary SLG, Sister Mary Paul SLG, A. M. Allchin (1973, 3/2022)
FP43	*The Power of the Name: The Jesus Prayer in Orthodox Spirituality*	Kallistos Ware (1974)
FP46	*Prayer and Contemplation* and *Distractions are for Healing*	Robert Llewelyn (1975, rev. 4/2025)
FP48	*The Wisdom of the Desert Fathers*	trans. Sister Benedicta Ward SLG (1975)
FP50	*Letters of Saint Antony the Great*	trans. Derwas Chitty (1975, 2/2021)
FP54	*From Loneliness to Solitude*	Roland Walls (1976)
FP55	*Theology and Spirituality*	Andrew Louth (1976, rev. 1978, 3/2024)
FP61	*Kabir: The Way of Love and Paradox*	Sister Rosemary SLG (1977)
FP62	*Anselm of Canterbury: A Monastic Scholar*	Sister Benedicta Ward SLG (1973, 2/2024)
FP67	*Mary and the Mystery of the Incarnation: An Essay on the Mother of God in the Theology of Karl Barth*	Andrew Louth (1977, 2/2024)
FP68	*Trinity and Incarnation in Anglican Tradition*	A. M. Allchin (1977, rev. 2/2025)
FP70	*Facing Depression*	Gonville ffrench-Beytagh (1978, 2/2020)
FP71	*The Single Person*	Philip Welsh (1979)
FP72	*The Letters of Ammonas, Successor of St Antony*	trans. Derwas Chitty, introd. Sebastian Brock (1979, 2/2023)
FP74	*George Herbert, Priest and Poet*	Kenneth Mason (1980)
FP75	*A Study of Wisdom: Three Tracts by the Author of The Cloud of Unknowing*	trans. Clifton Wolters (1980)
FP81	*The Psalms: Prayer Book of the Bible*	Dietrich Bonhoeffer, trans. Sister Isabel SLG (1982, rev. 3/2025)
FP82	*Prayer & Holiness: The Icon of Man Renewed in God*	Dumitru Stăniloae (1982, rev. 2/2023)
FP85	*Walter Hilton: Eight Chapters on Perfection & Angels' Song*	trans. Rosemary Dorward (1983, rev. 3/2024)
FP88	*Creative Suffering*	Iulia de Beausobre (1989)
FP90	*Bringing Forth Christ: Five Feasts of the Child Jesus by St Bonaventure*	trans. Eric Doyle OFM (1984, 3/2024)
FP92	*Gentleness in John of the Cross*	Thomas Kane (1985, rev. 2/2025)
FP94	*Saint Gregory Nazianzen: Selected Poems*	trans. John McGuckin (1986, 2/2024)
FP95	*The World of the Desert Fathers: Stories and Sayings from the Anonymous Series of the Apophthegmata Patrum*	trans. Columba Stewart OSB (1986, 2/2020)
FP104	*Growing Old with God*	Timothy N. Rudd (1988, 2/2020)
FP106	*Julian Reconsidered*	Kenneth Leech, Sister Benedicta Ward SLG (1988/ rev. 2/2024)

FP108	*The Unicorn: Meditations on the Love of God*	Harry Galbraith Miller (1989)
FP109	*The Creativity of Diminishment*	Sister Anke (1990)
FP110	*Called to be Priests*	Hugh Wybrew (1989, updated 2/2024)
FP111	*A Kind of Watershed: An Anglican Lay View of Sacramental Confession*	
		Christine North (1990, updated 2/2022)
FP116	*Jesus, the Living Lord*	Bishop Michael Ramsey (1992)
FP120	*The Monastic Letters of Saint Athanasius the Great*	
		trans. and introd. Leslie Barnard (1994, 2/2023)
FP122	*The Hidden Joy*	Sister Jane SLG, ed. Dorothy Sutherland (1994)
FP124	*Prayer of the Heart: An Approach to Silent Prayer and Prayer in the Night*	
		Alexander Ryrie (1995, 3/2020)
FP126	*Evelyn Underhill, Anglican Mystic: Two Centenary Essays*	
		A. M. Allchin, Bishop Michael Ramsey (1977, rev. 4/2025)
FP127	*Apostolate and the Mirrors of Paradox*	
		Sydney Evans, ed. Andrew Linzey & Brian Horne (1996)
FP128	*The Wisdom of Saint Isaac the Syrian*	Sebastian Brock (1997)
FP129	*Saint Thérèse of Lisieux: Her Relevance for Today*	Sister Eileen Mary SLG (1997)
FP130	*Expectations: Five Addresses for Those Beginning Ministry*	Sister Edmée SLG (1997, 2/2024)
FP131	*Scenes from Animal Life: Fables for the Enneagram Types*	
		Waltraud Kirschke, trans. Sister Isabel SLG (1998)
FP132	*Praying the Word of God: The Use of Lectio Divina*	Charles Dumont OCSO (1999)
FP133	*Love Unknown: Meditations on the Death and Resurrection of Jesus*	
		John Barton (1999, 2/2024)
FP134	*The Hidden Way of Love: Jean-Pierre de Caussade's Spirituality of Abandonment*	
		Barry Conaway (1999, rev. 2/2025)
FP135	*Shepherd and Servant: The Spiritual Theology of Saint Dunstan*	Douglas Dales (2000)
FP137	*Pilgrimage of the Heart*	Sister Benedicta Ward SLG (2001)
FP138	*Mixed Life*	Walter Hilton, trans. Rosemary Dorward (2001, enlarged rev. 3/2024)
FP139	*In the Footsteps of the Lord: The Teaching of Abba Isaiah of Scetis*	
		John Chryssavgis, Luke Penkett (2001, 2/2023)
FP140	*A Great Joy: Reflections on the Meaning of Christmas*	Kenneth Mason (2001)
FP141	*Bede and the Psalter*	Sister Benedicta Ward SLG (2002, 2/2024)
FP142	*Abhishiktananda: A Memoir of Dom Henri Le Saux*	Murray Rogers, David Barton (2003)
FP143	*Friendship in God: The Encounter of Evelyn Underhill & Sorella Maria of Campello*	
		A. M. Allchin (2003, rev. 2/2025)
FP144	*Christian Imagination in Poetry and Polity: Some Anglican Voices from Temple to Herbert*	
		Bishop Rowan Williams (2004)
FP145	*The Reflections of Abba Zosimas: Monk of the Palestinian Desert*	
		trans. and introd. John Chryssavgis (2005, 3/2022)
FP146	*The Gift of Theology: The Trinitarian Vision of Ann Griffiths and Elizabeth of Dijon*	
		A. M. Allchin (2005)
FP147	*Sacrifice and Spirit*	Bishop Michael Ramsey (2005)
FP148	*Saint John Cassian on Prayer*	trans. A. M. Casiday (2006, 2/2024)
FP149	*Hymns of Saint Ephrem the Syrian*	trans. Mary Hansbury (2006, 2/2024)
FP150	*Suffering: Why All this Suffering? What Do I Do about It?*	
		Reinhard Körner OCD, trans. Sister Avis Mary SLG (2006)
FP151	*A True Easter: The Synod of Whitby 664 AD*	Sister Benedicta Ward SLG (2007, 2/2023)
FP152	*Prayer as Self-Offering*	Alexander Ryrie (2007)
FP153	*From Perfection to the Elixir: How George Herbert Fashioned a Famous Poem*	
		Benedick de la Mare (2008, 2/2024)

FP154	*The Jesus Prayer: Gospel Soundings*	Sister Pauline Margaret CHN (2008)
FP155	*Loving God Whatever: Through the Year with Sister Jane*	Sister Jane SLG (2006)
FP156	*Prayer and Meditation for a Sleepless Night*	SISTERS OF THE LOVE OF GOD (1993, 3/2024)
FP157	*Being There: Caring for the Bereaved*	John Porter (2009)
FP158	*Learn to Be at Peace: The Practice of Stillness*	Andrew Norman (2010)
FP159	*From Holy Week to Easter*	George Pattison (2010)
FP160	*Strength in Weakness: The Scandal of the Cross*	John W. Rogerson (2010)
FP161	*Augustine Baker: Frontiers of the Spirit*	Victor de Waal (2010, rev. 2/2025)
FP162	*Out of the Depths*	Gonville ffrench-Beytagh; epilogue Wendy Robinson (1990, 2/2010)
FP163	*God and Darkness: A Carmelite Perspective*	Gemma Hinricher OCD, trans. Sister Avis Mary SLG (2010)
FP164	*The Gift of Joy*	Curtis Almquist SSJE (2011)
FP165	*'I Have Called You Friends': Suggestions for the Spiritual Life Based on the Farewell Discourses of Jesus*	Reinhard Körner OCD (2012)
FP166	*Leisure*	Mother Mary Clare SLG (2012)
FP167	*Carmelite Ascent: An Introduction to Saint Teresa and Saint John of the Cross*	Mother Mary Clare SLG (1973, rev. 2/2012)
FP168	*Ann Griffiths and Her Writings*	Llewellyn Cumings (2012)
FP169	*The Our Father*	Sister Benedicta Ward SLG (2012)
FP171	*The Spiritual Wisdom of the Syriac Book of Steps*	Robert A. Kitchen (2013)
FP172	*The Prayer of Silence*	Alexander Ryrie (2012)
FP173	*On Tour in Byzantium: Excerpts from The Spiritual Meadow of John Moschus*	Ralph Martin SSM (2013)
FP174	*Monastic Life*	Bonnie Thurston (2016)
FP175	*Shall All Be Well? Reflections for Holy Week*	Graham Ward (2015)
FP176	*Solitude and Communion: Papers on the Hermit Life*	ed. A. M. Allchin (2015)
FP177	*The Prayers of Jacob of Serugh*	ed. Mary Hansbury (2015)
FP178	*The Monastic Hours of Prayer*	Sister Benedicta Ward SLG (2016)
FP179	*The Desert of the Heart: Daily Readings with the Desert Fathers*	trans. Sister Benedicta Ward SLG (2016)
FP180	*In Company with Christ: Lent, Palm Sunday, Good Friday & Easter to Pentecost*	Sister Benedicta Ward SLG (2016)
FP181	*Lazarus: Come Out! Reflections on John 11*	Bonnie Thurston (2017)
FP182	*Unknowing & Astonishment: Meditations on Faith for the Long Haul*	Christopher Scott (2018)
FP183	*Pondering, Praying, Preaching: Romans 8*	Bonnie Thurston (2019, 2/2021)
FP184	*Shem'on the Graceful: Discourse on the Solitary Life*	trans. and introd. Mary Hansbury (2020)
FP185	*God Under My Roof: Celtic Songs and Blessings*	Esther de Waal (2020)
FP186	*Journeying with the Jesus Prayer*	James F. Wellington (2020)
FP187	*Poet of the Word: Re-reading Scripture with Ephraem the Syrian*	Aelred Partridge OC (2020)
FP188	*Identity and Ritual*	Alan Griffiths (2021)
FP189	*River of the Spirit: The Spirituality of Simon Barrington-Ward*	Andy Lord (2021)
FP190	*Prayer and the Struggle against Evil*	John Barton, Daniel Lloyd, James Ramsay, Alexander Ryrie (2021)
FP191	*Dante's Spiritual Journey: A Reading of the Divine Comedy*	Tony Dickinson (2021)
FP192	*Jesus the Undistorted Image of God*	John Townroe (2022)

FP193	*Our Deepest Desire: Prayer, Fasting & Almsgiving in the Writings of Saint Augustine of Hippo*	Sister Susan SLG (2022)
FP194	*Lent with George Herbert*	Tony Dickinson (2022)
FP195	*Four Ways to the Cross*	Tony Dickinson (2022)
FP196	*Anselm of Canterbury, Teacher of Prayer*	Sister Benedicta Ward SLG (2022)
FP197	*With One Heart and Mind: Prayers out of Stillness*	Anthony Kemp (2023)
FP198	*Sayings of the Urban Fathers & Mothers*	James Ashdown (2023)
FP199	*Doors*	Sister Raphael SLG (2023)
FP200	*Monastic Vocation*	SISTERS OF THE LOVE OF GOD, Bishop Rowan Williams (2021)
FP201	*An Ecology of the Heart: Faith Through the Climate Crisis*	Duncan Forbes (2023)
FP202	*'In the image of the Image': Gregory of Nyssa's Opposition to Slavery*	Adam Couchman (2023)
FP203	*Gregory of Nyssa and the Sins of Asia Minor*	Jonathan Farrugia (2023)
FP204	*Discovery*	Arthur Bell (2023)
FP205	*Living Healing: the Spirituality of Leanne Payne*	Andy Lord (2023)
FP206	*Still Listening: Sowing the Seeds of the Jesus Prayer*	Bruce Batstone CJN (2023)
FP207	*Julian of Norwich: Four Essays to Commemorate 650 Years of the Revelations of Divine Love*	Bishop Graham Usher, Father Colin CSWG, Sister Elizabeth Ruth Obbard OC, Mother Hilary Crupi OJN (2023)
FP208	*TIME*	Dumitru Stăniloae, Kallistos Ware (2023)
FP209	*Pearls of Life: A Lifebelt for the Spirit*	Tony Dickinson (2024)
FP210	*The Way and the Truth and the Life: An Exploration by a Follower of the Way*	James Ramsay (2024)
FP211	*Cosmos, Crisis & Christ: Essays of Wendy Robinson*	Wendy Robinson (2024)
FP212	*Towards a Theology of Psychotherapy: The Spirituality of Wendy Robinson*	Andrew Louth (2024)
FP213	*Immersed in God and the World: Living Priestly Ministry*	Andy Lord (2024)
FP214	*The Road to Emmaus: A Sculptor's Journey through Time*	Rodney Munday (2024)
FP215	*Prayer Too Deep for Words*	Sister Edmée SLG (2024)
FP216	*The Prayers of St Isaac of Nineveh*	Sebastian Brock (2024)
FP217	*Two Medieval English Saints: Cuthbert and Alban*	Sister Benedicta Ward SLG (2024)
FP218	*Encountering the Depths*	Mother Mary Clare SLG (1981, rev. 3/2024)
FP219	*Conflict and Concord*	Sister Susan SLG, Bishop Humphrey Southern, Bronwen Neil, Sister Rosemary SLG, Sister Clare-Louise SLG (2024)
FP220	*Divine Love in the Song of Songs*	Sister Edmée SLG (2024)
FP221	*Zeal for the Faith: An Introduction to Christian-Muslim Dialogue*	Tony Dickinson (2024)
FP222	*Bernard & Abelard*	Sister Edmée SLG (2024)
FP223	*Eliot's Transitions: T. S. Eliot's Search for Identity and the Society of the Sacred Mission at Kelham Hall*	Vincent Strudwick (2024)
FP224	*Landscape, Soul and Spirit: Ecology, Prayer and Robert Macfarlane*	Andy Lord (2025)
FP225	*Our Home is in God*	John Townroe (2025)
FP226	*Signs of the Times: A Brief Survey of the Bible's Apocalyptic Writings*	Tony Dickinson (2025)
FP227	*And We Shall be Changed: Christian Reflections on Death and Dying*	James Ramsay (2025)

www.slgpress.co.uk

Contemplative Poetry Series

CP1	*Amado Nervo: Poems of Faith and Doubt*	trans. John Gallas (2021)
CP2	*Anglo-Saxon Poets: The High Roof of Heaven*	trans. John Gallas (2021)
CP3	*Middle English Poets: Where Grace Grows Ever Green*	ed. John Gallas (2021)
CP4	*The Voice inside Our Home: Selected Poems*	Edward Clarke (2022)
CP5	*Women & God: Drops in the Sea of Time*	trans. and ed. John Gallas (2022)
CP6	*Gabrielle de Coignard & Vittoria Colonna: Fly Not Too High*	trans. John Gallas (2022)
CP7	*Chancing on Sanctity: Selected Poems*	James Ramsay (2022)
CP8	*Gabriela Mistral: This Far Place*	trans. John Gallas (2023)
CP9	*Henry Vaughan & George Herbert: Divine Themes and Celestial Praise*	ed. Edward Clarke (2023)
CP10	*Love Will Come with Fire: Anthology*	Sisters of the Love of God (2023)
CP11	*Touchpapers: Anthology*	coll. and trans. John Gallas (2023)
CP12	*Seasons of my Soul: Selected Poems*	Clare McKerron (2023)
CP13	*Reinhard Sorge: Take Flight to God*	trans. John Gallas (2024)
CP14	*Embertide: Encountering Saint Frideswide*	Romola Parish (2024)
CP15	*Thomas Campion: Made All of Light*	ed. and introd. Julia Craig-McFeely (2024)
CP16	*When God Hides: Selected Poems*	Joseph Evans (2025)

Vestry Guides

VG1	*The Visiting Minister: How to Welcome Visiting Clergy to Your Church*	Paul Monk (2021)
VG2	*Help! No Minister! or Please Take the Service*	Paul Monk (2022)
VG3	*The Liturgy of the Eucharist: An Introductory Guide*	Paul Monk (2024)

www.slgpress.co.uk

The Sisters of the Love of God is an Anglican community of women religious living a contemplative monastic life.

To learn more about the Community and the Convent of the Incarnation at Fairacres, Oxford, see our website www.slg.org.uk.

As well as supporting those seeking to follow a vocation to the monastic life, the Community has a number of forms of association for those who feel drawn to share in the Sisters' life of prayer:
Fellowship of the Love of God, Companions,
Priests Associate or Oblate Sisters.

For more information email sisters@slg.org.uk or write to
The Reverend Mother, Convent of the Incarnation, Parker Street,
Oxford, OX4 1TB, UK.